The Sky Will Overtake You

Also by Marcia Falk

Poetry

Inner East: Illuminated Poems and Blessings
Poems accompanied by the author's art

My Son Likes Weather

It Is July in Virginia

This Year in Jerusalem

Translations

The Spectacular Difference: Selected Poems of Zelda
Translations from the 20th-century Hebrew poet, with introduction and
notes

With Teeth in the Earth: Selected Poems of Malka Heifetz Tussman
Translations from the Yiddish, with introduction and notes

The Song of Songs: Love Lyrics from the Bible
Translation from the biblical Hebrew, with introduction

The Song of Songs: A New Translation and Interpretation
Translation from the biblical Hebrew, with introduction, notes, and
commentary

Am I Also You?
Translations from the 20th-century Yiddish poet Malka Heifetz Tussman

Liturgy

Night of Beginnings: A Passover Haggadah
A poetic re-creation of the traditional haggadah, in Hebrew and English

*The Days Between: Blessings, Poems, and Directions of the Heart for the Jewish
High Holiday Season*
A poetic re-creation of Hebrew and English prayers for Rosh Hashanah,
Yom Kippur, and the days between them

*The Book of Blessings: New Jewish Prayers for Daily Life, the Sabbath, and the
New Moon Festival*
A poetic re-creation of Hebrew and English prayers from a nonhierarchical,
inclusive perspective, with commentary

The Sky Will Overtake You

poems

Marcia Falk

Scarlet Tanager
BOOKS
Oakland, California

Cover painting, detail: *Sky and Sea #18*, soft pastel on Somerset archival paper, by Marcia Falk
Copyright © 2018 by Marcia Lee Falk

Cover and interior design: Jess Morphew
jessmorphewdesign.com

Published by Scarlet Tanager Books
P.O. Box 20906
Oakland, CA 94620
scarlettanager.com

ISBN 978-1-7345313-8-1
Library of Congress Control Number (LCCN): 2024942492

For Steven

And for Abraham Gilead (Abby)

And in beloved memory of Sam
Samuel J. Falk, *z"l*

Contents

Time Telling

Seven Infinities of Grief

Foreword

Marcia Falk and I go back. We go way back, to thickets by the Susquehanna, tangled terms of service to our working lives and private loves. We were devourers of the arts.

What marked our spirits then, I think, were passion in expressive values, sense expressed as sensuality, and vehemence in service to our forms, which always hungered for transforming. Age itself becomes a force, as some emotions turn to their devotions. Acts become their practices.

And the impressions flourish where expression quiets down. Where once I recognized in Marcia's work a similar barometer for feeling, feel for taste, and taste for texture (both of us devoted to our graphic arts), in later works of Marcia's I am taken by the space. The no quiescent to the yes. In short, the quiet.

Flash of surfaces is giving way to depth of insight. Forms themselves resist the forge, the streaming needs, the press and rush.

The canvas gleams. For clarity, she lifts the brush.

—Heather McHugh

The Grammar of Clouds

The Muse Finally Speaks

You don't need me, she says.
The sky will overtake you—
a stunning event each time you step outside.
You do not have to call up the thousand configurations
of emptiness and cloud.
On its own, without the workings of your mind,
the sky will impart color and contour
to flatland, house, and hill.
Memory, imagination—they are nothing
compared to the sheer, simple fact of it:
the indelible, inviolate fact
of sky.

The Feast

The laden arms of the oak, the elm,
and the agitated hunger of the small jays,

the fat globes of white sugarmum
where bees suck love,

and you
in the morning shade,

tasting the new day, sharp
and alive on your tongue,

are a chorus that says,
Indulge! The world is abundant—

this loving, dying world
to which we are given,

out of which we have come—
O body of the world,

eat with joy
the body of the world!

Rosh Hashanah

Today is the birthday of the world
but the world knows nothing
of this invention.

The world just keeps moving about itself,
buzzing and humming, exulting and keening,
birthing and being born,

while the mind keeps on its own way—
form-craving, metaphor-making,
over and over, giving birth and being born.

It

is not a trance, not
a visitation.

It is nothing.

Just

the mind gently sweeping thought away
until the window is blank.

When it is over, you feel emptied,
a little stunned.

Then all at once, the noise returns
and the scrambling to sort it out.

You do not decide when this will happen.
You do not get to choose when it is gone.

I know, this isn't telling you anything.
It's just my need to put it down,
but see—

it
is already gone.

Ashes the moment,
its memory—

a tower made of water.

Morning

It's just as you almost remember—

light from below, slowly
opening into blue,

streak of charcoal hovering
on the horizon, lingering,

the day seeping upwards
into sky,

spilling through doors and windows
onto tables and floors and walls

in every room,
unstintingly.

You have decided to enjoy your hunger,

to say, *How great are Thy works*,
how goodly Thy tents,

even though
there is no *Thou* for you.

Your regrets are many and persistent;
they have dug their home in you.

In spite, you have decided
to love your life.

Geranium

What color is the geranium in the sunlight?
In the rain?
Outside, in the windowbox?
Inside, on the windowsill?

Alone? Beside the next one?

When you look up? Two hours later?
When the neighbor opens her window?
When a bird swoops between the buildings,
arcing past the tan wall and the gray wall,
the red- and blue-tiled roofs?

While you're waiting for something to happen?
When you think nothing is happening?

After long absence?
While longing? When grieving?

What color is it when you're hungry?
Before you're awake?

What color when the bells begin to ring?
Just before they ring?
The moment after they stop ringing?

When you stop thinking about the question?

After you've forgotten the question?

After you stop staring at the flower's hot eye,
which glares back at you like fire,
refusing to answer?

Like Buds

Such gratitude as might be held
by the widespreading arms
of the most noble trees—

where can it go if not up
to the heavens,

or to the depths of earth, which yields
to every step,
commanding nothing?

Or perhaps it has no destination,
no reason beyond itself for being,

like buds that cannot help
but open—

                    Oh,
what's the difference,
what's this need to know?

Let it go wherever,
to burst the seams of meanness,
puncture the blistering regrets,

letting loose the grieving
to nowhere

or somewhere,
whether or not you know its name.

The Gift

Sitting before a row of green and yellow lettuces
with no desire
but to render them gently;

when the light dips under a cloud,
a blue shadow stirs the faces
of their generous leaves.

Last night you dreamt you were forgiven
by an old friend with whom you had quarreled,
and today you are almost peaceful

watching a blue truck lumber away
past the turn in the woods,
woods just beginning to turn from green,

while clouds smooth the ruffled edges
here and there
partway through your life.

Summer Storm

All the peonies crashed to the ground in last night's rain.
They just opened yesterday, and already today
their reds and pinks are strewn across the lawn.

The other flowers in the garden held their ground,
their petals clinging fiercely to their stems—
the thick-stalked pelargoniums, of course,
but also the buttercups and pansies.
The ones we didn't plant—
the wild asters, the yarrow, the clover—
are accustomed to any weather,
nothing daunts them.
As for the daylilies—
they seemed to welcome the downpour,
catching and holding it all morning in their orange cups.

Why do only the giant globes of peony—
the most spectacular flower in the garden—
succumb this way?
Are their petals sewn together with air?
When the mid-night wind carries off their delicate scent,
is it too much for them to bear?
Do the glorious heads fall
because the hearts come undone,
or are they just too laden with beauty
not to fall?

Awakening

A sudden thud at the window
stops the morning
from veering off to a forgettable place.

Where were you before you looked up
to see the smashed feathers,
the smudge of blood on the pane?

Open Wings

If you draw a bird from her nest,
away from her elaborate labors,
seducing her with seed—

If you draw the curtains apart
so she sees your cupped hand
beckoning at the sill—

If you draw water to fill the stone bath
where she drinks and preens
and washes her wings—

when she comes, open-winged,
her throat filled with music,
will she bring you back to yourself?

Before You Saw Him

You heard him,
invisible whirr in the bushes—

hummingbird?
bumblebee?

Or wind stirring the plum tree's
ruby-black leaves,

color foretelling
a sweet, dark taste

with a tough
sour skin?

What Do You Hear?

A bird that calls
five calls
and waits for its mate

A hum of distant traffic
that might be ocean
or wind

A caw
      like a door
                  swinging open

The foghorns warn without cease:
Here is rock, here
is the edge

When the mate answers,
the bird calls again
five times

The trees look too large to creak,
but they do
because of the wind

When the wind is up,
even the small grasses
find their low voice

Nothing to be made
of any of it. No lessons
in the afternoon sounds

Only the music
as the sounds
                drift
                        apart
and float back together into silence

Listen

In the clearing
where the mind flowers
and the world sprouts up at every side,

listen
for the sound in the bushes
behind the grass.

Bones

How much of the body leaves us
while we are still here, observing?

The hair loses its color and falls from the scalp;
the skin—from too much handling of the elements,
too much dipping in and soaking up
the world's potions and poisons—
dries to a dull parchment, ready at a touch to crack.
The bone grows porous and hollow.
One day you wade into the ocean and it throws you back,
smashing your coccyx against the rocks.

Only the body's yearning remains whole,
in sleep and in conscious day,
and wherever you want most to let it go.
There, especially fiercely.

What Do You Have?

Not this earth, not even dust—
Not yours, caw invisible crows
like doors swinging shut

Not your memories, rising
and burning in the air
like leaf-dew in sun

Not your thoughts,
darting in and out
like hummingbirds in the blossoms

Only this bit of time,
like clouds unforming—
even as you point to it,

gone

Dictated in Sleep
by an Anonymous Source

Our lives are lent to us
and taken back,
the days laid out like jewels
on a merchant's table,
to be sorted and chosen.
As though they were ours to choose.

As though they were ours to take.
As though by choosing
we could make them ours.
As though by having
we could keep.
As though having itself
were a kind of keeping.

From where does it come,
and how, and when—
the knowing that none of it is ours,
that our life is delusion,
a hoax, a trick
to make us believe we're here?

Drinking Tea

Drinking the first tea of the morning,
the taste bittersweet on your tongue,
light arcing across the south window,
clouds releasing the steam of daybreak,
then burning away—
you see, once more, how tea changes over time,
like people.
You think you know its qualities,
and then you don't.
Even after you've strained off the leaves,
tea dust continues to steep at the bottom,
so that your second sip is not like the first.
Sometimes the taste becomes richer,
sometimes drier, even harsh.
Your tongue is aware
even when your thoughts drift away.

Do not drink quickly.
Drinking tea is not about quenching a thirst,
though it may have started that way.

But how can you help wanting all of it,
wanting it now?

You are no longer talking about tea.

Come back to the first cup,
take the first sip.

The Three Disciplines Necessary
to the Practice of Sumi-e

Adapted from a source long forgotten

Composing the Mind

Before one touches brush to paper
the mind is like the surface of a lake.
Let no shadow be cast.
Approach the task with frankness.
A genuine work
may happen.

Correcting the Posture

While painting, the body is held straight
but not stiff,
like trees that catch the wind above a cliff.
This posture dispels disturbing thoughts.
The mind is cleared
for perception.

Breathing

Breathing is adjusted to the physical
qualities of the object to be drawn.
Air
has its own densities.

Observe the swallow about to leave the tree.

Begin now.

Five Instructions for Ink Wash Painting

After the Ming dynasty master Zhang Hong

Do not start with an image in the mind.
Let the brush take you
where it wants to go.
Coax the eye to come along.

When you paint a waterfall, you are not painting the water.
You are painting around the water.
Suddenly the waterfall appears.

You can paint dark over light.
You cannot paint light over dark.
When the line dries, it will lighten.

Each stroke affects the whole.
See what is there.
Imagine
what will come.

The brushwork itself is utmost.
Even when you don't notice it.
The little touches that you don't notice
give the painting life.

Observe the tree after the swallow leaves.

Begin now.

How to Paint the Sky

Begin with white.

White is the paper left untouched.
White is what you do not do.

Hold back your craving hand.
White is you turning away.

Turning back, you see
a thousand colors.

Lift your brush
and choose.

White becomes the clouds
whose shapes reveal the sky.

Warning

"Because of recent storms and damage to the shoreline, the ocean
may contain debris that presents a significant safety hazard."
—Sign posted on the Santa Monica shore

The ocean is contaminated with land:
Enter at your own risk.
A tree that once overhung a cliff
may pierce the belly
of the next wave. Any minute,
someone's house may float up in pieces
to stab your ankles.

Here on the sand,
the contract to a thirty-year-old marriage
has washed up, translucent,
at the spot where your feet
sink in their own impermanence.

As you edge toward the water,
former fishtank dwellers
rush to your toes.
See how fat and healthy
the fish have grown.
The feel of their soft mouths
nibbling on your skin
entices, emboldens you.

You step more deliberately,
watching the knife-edged horizon
glint gold, then disappear.
The sky lifts its diamond-studded neck,
opening its throat to you.

You wade out farther,
rise onto the sure, sleek back
of a rolling wave,
your body light, all light, as it enters
the jeweled, devastated cave.

Suburb

This light that rises
from the bushes fat with shadow
and from bulging yellow-green lawns,
flattening maple trees against the sky,

light that flashes
through poles, along wires,
through tips of sparrowbeaks,
and at the narrow edge of fires,

this light that ripples
over the awnings of supper
where ice in beaded glasses
ignites, and slides away like suns,

light that fades
in blueing rooms of evening,
flowered rooms of cribs and cradles
where infants' faces shine like moons,

disappears
as we rock, benignly,
adrift on a sea of porches,
while the earth makes its next move.

We Know Her

We see her in the shimmering blades,
their bright green waving on the hill,

and hear her through the cottonwoods, the aspens,
flying free through their leafy crowns.

We breathe her as she lifts to the sky
the scents of the newly furrowed field,

and feel her touching our forehead
in our fevered dreams.

Only the taste of her emptiness
is saved for tomorrow,

remembered honey of mother's milk,
manna of our longing—

wind.

Earth

See how it falls, unhurried,
between your fingers,
leaving traces of itself in the creases—

wood and acid, flower and metal
in the crescents of the nails.

See how, when you dig in its darkness,
it settles its weight in your hand,
at home with its child,

and how, when you lay it back
around the newly planted roots,
patting it down with the flat of your palm,

it leaves you again,
without resisting,

the way hair, skin, sight, mind
go, quietly, cell by cell,
so gently you can only imagine

to what soft bed, what body
you are being delivered.

Eden

She planted a garden, lush, chaotic.
The overflow put her at ease,
as though

everything were there,
waiting
for her to form it.

She never tired of its smallest gestures—
falling petal, wind-lifted leaf,
shift of shadow on grass—

nor of its larger openings and closings,
the foldings and unfoldings
of branches and vines.

How easily it all came and went,
how it made time pass easily, as though
there were nothing left in the world

to be concerned with,
no reason on earth to leave
or to stay.

In a Lawn Chair

Sitting by the edge of the pond,
Lillian rests after a week of guests.
She has swept the oak floors along the grain,
the tables are clean of crumbs,
linens flap softly in the breeze.
Lillian gazes at the pond,
at the small waves uncurling from its quiet center
and settling on the crinkling shore.

She has lived here 84 years,
long enough to see the 200-year-old farmhouse
fill with children, and grandchildren,
and, years later, empty out again.
She was here to see the pond dug out of hard ground
and filled with trout, who multiplied.
She has watched the children swim and row and fish.
And she has seen the water lilies—
a gift from well-meaning guests—
take over the pond and multiply and clot its surface.
The pond is good now only for watching.

On mild days, Lillian sits
and watches the pond.

Imagining Sappho's Morning

The sweet apple reddens on a high branch
high upon highest, missed by the applepickers:
No, they didn't miss, so much as couldn't touch . . .
            —Trans. Diane Rayor

—couldn't reach, couldn't come near,
not near enough even
to smell the ripe fragrance
or hear the hummingbirds whirring,
their bodies glittering in the daylight
like scattered jewels from a necklace
that came unstrung the night before
when it dropped from her neck
(her lover's hand cupping her neck,
fingers catching in her hair,
the string snapping, the beads spilling
across the marble floor)—

Was this the story she began to tell
the next morning in the grove
(or was it in her room, an ordinary room
with a small writing-table and an empty fruit bowl,
empty cup, unmade bed, open doorway?),
watching the birds take their greedy fill
in the branches that no one, not even she,
the greatest poet of desire, could touch?

The Cellist Tastes Music

"Professional musician distinguishes intervals with her tongue."
—*Nature*, 2 March 2005

Play a minor sixth—
heavy cream fills her mouth;
a major sixth—
only milk is on her tongue.
Mirror images on the scale,
such as the minor second and the major seventh,
taste alike to her.
The dissonant tritone tastes disgusting.
An octave has no flavor
because its two notes are the same—
a match made in heaven, or hell.
But the fourth—ah, the fourth—
tastes like freshly mown grass.
She has these sensations
even while eating
or seeing words on a screen.
Show her the word *sweet* and play a major second—
she still tastes *bitter*.

What if I could taste music,
hear pictures, touch smells?
If my body were so liquid, so porous
it could not keep separate all its nerves and cells,
each doing the unique task
for which it so perfectly evolved?

Would images leap from the canvas
and settle on my ears? my fingers? my tongue?
Would words float away into sea?

Would the world beckon
or retreat?
Would I grasp more of it than I do today
when only a trickle of world
seeps through my skin?

Would I be ignited with sensation?

Or would I dissolve
into the flood of being
out of which I came?

The Grammar of Clouds

Some mornings, the clouds themselves
are a source of radiance,
the blue—merely a backdrop.

You are held
by their quiet shifting,
the slow, easy sway
of their clusterings and partings.

You follow the sky
as it spells out a story.
The hours overflow
with a saturating dailiness.

Other mornings, you wake
from one sleep to the next,
the weight of half-remembered dreams
still heavy on your eyes.

Days like these are a story
waiting to be told,
and you alone
are the teller.

The clouds—
a white robe
enfolding a dark confusion.

Light on the Larch

Light on the larch!
Light on the birch!

Light on the evergreen!
Light on the thousand greens of summer!

Light on the buzz and swarm,
on the honk, trill, swoosh, and thud,

light on the rush and rustle and whistle
and the music that stings the skin,

light on the miniscule motions
sketching the shape of the wind,

light on the cloud's curling vapor
and the tree-forms gathering

and darkening the horizon
at dusk.

Like Bells

Who can say that the light is not happiness
in the green of the leaves, the fern?

Who can say that joy is not the fern
opening to the low arms of pine?

Who can say that the wind lightly tossing the fern,
lifting the perfect arc of its frond to the sky,

where the smell of pine drifts over the narrow creek,
toward you, in a splatter of shadow

cast from the distant top branches
of the ever-greening redwood tree

is not the clear sound of water
spilling over the rocks like bells?

That Which Flows

That which flows
from eye to window
from tree to sky
from bird to bird
from hand to pen
from ink to paper
from paper to earth
from earth to tree
from tree to window
from window to eye
from eye to cloud
from cloud to cloud
from cloud to cloud
from cloud to leaf
from green to red
from green to yellow
from yellow to red
from sky to lake
from blue to blue
from lake to sky
will not be stilled
will not be slowed
will not be quickened
will not be hastened
will not wait
for the Messiah to come.

Time Telling

At Six

Under the shipwrecks of porcelain knickknacks,
drowned in the showers of cellophane flowers,
choked in the spume of an ancient perfume,
something's buried in Mama's basement.

Look here's the photo that fades in your fingers,
the picture unpeeling itself from the plaster
on walls behind wallboards beneath the small stairwell
where you can hide too in Mama's basement.

You're getting your dress stuck with sawdust and mousehair,
your hand-me-down dress with the crinoline lining
that was starch-spanking clean as a lie in the closet
one flight above Mama's basement.

You better beat it before Mama finds you,
go over to Suzy's for a mayonnaise sandwich
and watch the new baby, so still on the bedspread,
too little to roll away.

The Walls of My House

The walls of my house are thin
and full of tiny sounds.
My own skin is thin,
the veins break easily.
My scalp can be bruised by the teeth
of a fine-toothed comb
like the one Mama pulled through my knots
every school-morning, already late to work,
mumbling *goddamn nasty kid*—
although sometimes those mornings,
she'd stroke my eyes gently with wet cotton,
coaxing the gummy lids apart.

My neighbor lies in a coma,
impervious to fear,
not knowing her children, not dead.
Her daughter waits at her bedside
for permission to leave, or to stay.
Through the thin walls,
I hear her waiting;
already it's late.
She waits for a half-spoken word,
any blessing or curse,
as though waiting could coax
the sealed refusals open
or loosen the stiffened knots
our fragile bodies hold,

as though we could rise, forgiving,
from all our sleeps, and in partings
be made whole again.

Learning Grass

cheat   fescue   stipa
sedge   fatua   brome
rye grass   quaking grass
foxtail   rattlesnake grass

Growing up, I knew only lawn:
side-by-side, grass-green plots
mowed to a sheen,
enwrapped in topiary hedges,
bedecked with hot-pink azaleas,
yellow forsythia in season.

Don't step on the lawn.
Tell your brother to go cut the lawn.

The cheat calls out, *Don't pick me!*
The stipa says, *Don't break me.*
The foxtail says, *Watch out!*
I will stick you with my knife-sharp awns!

And a hundred awns
fly off on their mission,
tiny birds of prey on the wind:
seeds that will sprout
in the uncut trodden fields.

What Kept Me Standing

There are no birds in the backyard this morning—
no cobalt-blue jays, no red-breasted finches,
no yellow-bellied warblers.
Not even a plain gray sparrow.
There are no white clouds,
just a windowful of colorless sky.

My first painting teacher instructed me
not to rely on the imagination.
Work from life,
train your eye to see,
train your hand to remember.
I was twelve.
He didn't tell me what to do when life offered up
nothing I wanted to recall.

When I was almost thirteen
my father smacked me, hard, in the face,
with the front, then the back, of his hand.
This is what I have of it:
His wedding band making a clean, curved cut
across the bridge of my nose.
From the front door, where she stood, watching,
my mother calling to me—
Get over here.
Me, standing as still as I could,
watching the blood spill over my hot-pink sneakers,
pasting them to the sidewalk.

There are so many days when I cannot imagine
another life.

But sometimes without augur,
the birds come: jays, finches, warblers,
their blues and reds and yellows
crossing a transparent sky.

Then it all comes clear:
what he did and what she said,
what she didn't say and what he tried to say,
what kept me standing in place,
the years pooling at my feet.

Don't Trust Gardeners

When it comes to nature, despite what you'd think,
gardeners don't know all that much.
They tell you the birch will live ninety years,
and it's dead at twenty.
They say the Japanese maple you've planted in the back
will grow to five feet, no more,
and already it's nine feet tall,
you can barely see the brightest cardinals
alighting on the top branches.

And here's a question my gardener never answered:
Why do the very smallest birds—
which happen to be the prettiest,
the ones you most want to watch—
always go for the highest limbs of the tallest trees?

So I ask you: Why bother making a garden
when things only persist in having their own way?
All the planting and tending and uprooting and re-planting—
like everything else in life: You fix something
and another part breaks.

Take, for example, my personal obsession—cut flowers.
I arrange them in just the right combinations
of sizes and shapes and colors,
place them in vases and jars,
and match them up with the right spot in every room:
perfect!
And within a day it's time to cull the droopers
and plan out the whole business again.

If I didn't leave the house once in a while
nothing in it would get a rest.

And then there's my mother, bandaged and braced,
tucked in her hospital bed, stiff as a china doll.
Ninety-seven, and in just the last decade
she's broken nearly every bone in her shriveling body.
No sooner does one bone knit itself together
than the next one cracks
and mends even more slowly than the one before.
She's *dis*-integrating, no other way to put it—
less and less of her every day—
but clinging to each withering shred.

Meanwhile, her grandson goes on becoming
more and more his self,
stronger-limbed, stronger-willed.
Over the years, I watched the quirks creep in,
each as startling as the first diaper rash
or the acne that bloomed fifteen years later
on his milk-white face.
By the time the pimples backed off
a sparse dark stubble had replaced them.
Yet today—today he's a beauty.
Oh—
but where is the baby
who needed every minute of my day?

Take my word—
might as well forget about gardening.
No keeping anything the way you want it.
No keeping anything.

Learning to Play Basketball

Remembering my first lesson, how you set
the ball into my open hands, and raised
an eyebrow to the waiting net, how you
coaxed me to throw it easy, easy, eeeee
zee, diving with my knees, and letting go—

and how, later that night, we slid through weeds,
climbing the hill's path, falling as we rose,
the wet grass slipping from our cautious tread
and letting us go easy, easy
into the net of stars that hooped the earth.

As Though Everything
Were Not About to Change

In memory of my brother, Sam

1.

Sometimes when I am alone in the house,
I think I hear it moan and sigh,
speaking to me in the language of old buildings.
Then I hear a small crash, and I remember:
the rat.
My son's ingenious pet has sprung his cage again
and now he could be anywhere,
sharpening his teeth on the furniture,
bedding down in my clothing. Any minute
he might show up here,
ready to gnaw at the leg of my chair.
Or, worse, climb.

When I was very young, I believed that God
might appear like that—
anywhere, anytime, without warning.
I grew up and stopped believing in God,
but I remain skittish around quiet animals.

Of course, I know there is nothing
that cannot pounce.
Last year, in fact, I had news
that upended everything.
It shouldn't have come as such a shock—
people are nothing if not unpredictable—
but there it was:

Someone I was sure I knew,
I didn't.
A whole other life, lived
where I couldn't see it.

Over and over I have tried to figure out
where he—
where I—
was hiding.

2.

On days when the sky is filled with cloud—
cloud that is only a pulsing glow, without contour or color—
a particular kind of light finds its way
into the room where I make my tea.
This room is the smallest in the house, but it's all mine
and contains morning and evening, winter and summer,
coming and going.

I keep a photograph of my son on the ledge.
There's not much space for other things—
a few teacups, pencils, a clock,
and the anthurium I bought from a vendor on the street.
It wasn't flowering when I bought it;
the leaves were dried at the edges
and the roots poked through the cracks in the plastic pot.
It looked so pathetic, in fact, I bought a second plant, its twin,
and brought the two home together in a cardboard box—
the same box my son had used
to carry the baby rat home from the vivarium,
where the rats are raised as food for the snakes.

Forgive me. This business about the rats, the anthuriums—
it's not what I meant to tell you, which was only
how, this morning, the light drifts very slowly
through the cloud-filled window, so slowly
I can barely tell it is light
and not the seeping darkness of winter.

But then I see the anthurium growing transparent,
the pale buds beginning to glow
like a wink, like the start of a flame,
the tea turning golden in the cup,
and the hands of the clock sweeping smoothly
across its brightened face—

as though everything were not about to change
any moment.

Just in Case

Some of us are known by what we travel with, the things we won't leave behind when we leave home. I have a friend who takes his briefcase everywhere, risking its loss at gas stations, supermarkets, newsstands. I never see him open it, except at home.

Another friend carries two recipes on three-by-five cards when she flies crosscountry. One is for Basque fish soup, the other for bluefish with ginger. When she lands at a familiar place, such as the home of an old friend, such as me, she offers to cook dinner. She makes the soup or the bluefish and serves it to her hosts.

As for me, over the years I've grown attached to my blue wool sweater and wear it everywhere. Miraculously, it has all its buttons. I can't remember how I managed before I owned it.

And some people travel with *everything*. My brother used to take three suitcases and $300 in cash wherever he went. And a full set of tools, just in case anything went wrong.

Another View

Sitting in my usual spot under the pepper tree,
in deep shade, until my bones became so cold
I had to move to the far end of the garden
where bits of sun leaked through the tibouchina leaves.
From there, I saw the other side of grasses
whose colors and shapes I thought I knew.
I saw the curled brown edges of the calla lilies,
the gray insects lodged in their cups,
the snails clinging to the undersides.

I ran my fingers along the length of the Japanese maple
whose reddened leaves had dried to a brittle lace
that fell into my hands as I stroked it,
leaving the twigs naked and open
to anyone's touch.

Suddenly the lily stalks lit up like candles
and everything became visible.
Then I stopped thinking of cold
and wondered where the day was going
and how much of myself would go along.

First I Saw Him

Small, round, birch-colored,
almost hidden in the tree.

Then he saw me
and was gone.

But he visited again a moment later,
sang his song three times,

then once more,

while I stood, still,
in calf-high snow.

When he stopped,
the music settled everywhere.

But O
then there were two.

The Book and the Dog

It was a book I didn't love. But there I was, reading
by the footbridge at the bottom of Johnson's road,
when the snout of the white-haired dog
nudged itself toward my face.
Purely by instinct—
an instinct borrowed from someone else's body,
because, you see, I have always been afraid of dogs—
I reached out my hand to pat his head.
And when I looked up from the book
and saw him there, at my side, his head bobbing in the air,
all I thought was: *I am not afraid.*

A minute later, the dog was called away by its owner
who apologized for having disturbed my "quiet moment."
No, no, I insisted, wanting to tell her—
but how could I explain?

An ordinary dog,
a book whose words I'd already forgotten.

A Word

After reading Ted Kooser's "Old Lilacs"

Nickering. I found it in a poem
and had no idea, though I could imagine—
its music a mix of *niggling* and *picking*,
a small clatter of commerce passing hands.
But the poet had tied the word to *twigs*—
a nickering of twigs, he had written—
and so I thought *nudging* and *clicking*,
the sound of branches stirred by a light wind
at the start of spring, when the inchoate buds
test the air for kindness.
But still no.
Though at first glance the poet saw lilacs,
when he looked again, they became horses,
softly neighing: *nickering*.

Who would have guessed? Not I—
a girl raised in the suburbs, who had seen horses
only in Central Park, harnessed to hansom carriages,
the drivers gussied up like coachmen from another century
(top hats, boots, crimson vests, even in warm weather—
such fancy garb that before I could read
I thought the word for the coaches was *handsome*),
the passengers mostly tourists,
though some may just have been lovers,
impossibly hoping for a return to lost times.

Those horses, too, must have neighed,
though I can't recall actually hearing them
so taken was I with the sight of them,
genteely trotting or waiting their turn at the park's edge,
black masks side-blinding their sight.

Now, filling in the memory of their voices,
I like to imagine them *nickering*
the way they surely did once, in the fields of their youth,
calling each other out to play
in the flickering light of early spring.

Natural Excursions: Lust

When the jasmine blooms in my neighborhood
I go scouting,
and when I pass a hedgeful on the sidewalk
I tear off a piece of coiled, threadlike vine
full of needle-shaped buds.
The vine is tougher than it looks,
I have to fight for it.
I carry the sprig home in my pocket
and set it in a glass of water
where it unfolds slowly, the rose-pink tips
opening into translucent stars
whose perfume lingers long after they shrivel
into papery mementos of themselves.
The lining of my pocket, too,
smells like jasmine for days.

The jasmine is sweet, but my craving
has a sharp, bitter taste—
half-metal, half-stone.

Natural Excursions: Temptation

On cold, fog-heavy mornings,
three yellow apples call to me
from the neighbor's tree—

Come over here, come get us.
We are your crazy sisters,
the ones you've stopped speaking to.
We're still here, spying at your window—
a narrow pane, but big enough to watch you,
shuddering in your room,
nothing luring you into the day.

So come, come now, come over,
we are here,
waiting for you.

Natural Excursions: Rue

Had I arrived just a few moments sooner,
I might have witnessed the eclosing—
the splitting of the silk
and the sudden bright emergence,
the wings filling with blood,
the last drops of moisture shaken down.
And then, the first ascents.

As it was, I found a single black butterfly,
smaller than my thumb,
its underside speckled with baneberry blood,
its top striped with the piercing blue of a late-June sky.
When I followed it to a slab of mossy rock
I saw the whole throng of hatchlings—
one dozen, two dozen butterflies
all dipped in the same midnight ink.
All of them together
in a spot no bigger than a maple leaf—

There. Already there.

Hard Practice

I've made a new promise to myself:
Every day I will practice saying, *Enough*.

I'll leave the last strawberry in the bowl,
a few white slivers of peach.

I'll exit the museum
even before they announce the closing.

When I go for my morning walk,
I'll take beauty as it comes.
When I spy the first lilac of the season,
its dizzying fragrance filling the air around my face,
I won't hurry to turn the corner to see what's next.

A cancer is eating the fine brain
of my oldest childhood friend.
Sometimes, in the evenings,
her mother opens the family album,
touches lightly the photographs
of her thriving grandchildren.

Every day I'll practice saying, *Enough*.
It is enough.

The Guests

For SJR

On the eve of our betrothal,
they came to me:

the purple burdock with its hidden orange root,
the silver birch shivering in the green light of ferns,

the deer disappearing into the clefts of the hills,
the soft hair of your belly, like starry moss—

Oh, stay! Stay in your bodies,
fragile and lovely,

stay past the winding of the slender thread,
the halted talk of the birds.

Sonnet for the Wedding

We approach like children
in a grade-school play,
each line rehearsed,
each gesture on display.

Primped and practiced,
steadying our breath,
we discipline ourselves
not to think of death.

It's the word we do not say,
it's what we *not* say
over and over
as we take our vow,

going headstrong, body first
over the edge of now.

My Face

Three times since turning fifty, I've broken my face:
twice falling on the bulging sidewalks of my neighborhood,
once stepping into an elevator in a foreign city.
Up until then, my face had been mine.
Now I have scars: one on my upper lip, the other just above it
in the place the angel touches before we are born,
causing us to forget everything we knew.
And my nose—it changed course so recklessly each time I fell
that I no longer recall where it started out.

When I look in the mirror these days, I meet a stranger;
everything about her needs deciphering.
Is she kind? Yes, there is kindness there.
Does she have a sense of humor?
Oh yes! Just look at those lines near the corners of her eyes—
though some of them may have come from squinting
or from crying; it's hard to be sure.

In the old days, I took my face for granted.
The gray-blue color of the eyes,
the homely dark hollows beneath them,
the odd asymmetry of its shape,
the quick mutability of expression—
all were known to me and, hence, unrevealing.
Now I study my face and wonder:
Whose is it today?
Who is this stepping out of the shower
to reveal her permeable desires?
Who will step back from the mirror
and go with me into the day?

Who will be there when I wake
and when I sleep?
Who will answer when I cry out in joy,
when I call out in grief?
Who will keep me company and comfort me
when I finally become one
with all my faces
and attached to none of them?

Miscalculation

On my sixtieth birthday, I bought myself flowers
by the dozens—
roses, chrysanthemums, snapdragons,
foxglove, larkspur, lilies—everything
that caught my eye on the stands.
I thought, turning sixty,
I would fill the house with flowers—
a celebration, a gala!

But it quickly got out of hand:
the first week of my sixty-first year
given over to arranging and re-arranging,
cleaning and picking away,
removing the dead and the near-dead,
swooping up fallen petals,
plucking off withered leaves,
sweeping surfaces clean
of orange-staining pollen.
I had no peace—nothing
was ever right.
Finally I gave up,
tossed the whole mess out.

Then I wished I'd bought a single iris—
the flower that bursts open suddenly
when you're not watching
and burns itself out within a day,
its three blue flames
totally extinguished,
its perfection perfectly brief.

Looking Out at 70,
I Tell Myself It's No Different from 69

A lie.

Just look at the hummingbirds this morning
spinning furiously in the Chinese lantern tree.
How they go at the blood-red blossoms—
at them and *at* them—as if
this were the last of their thirst.

My Hair

Every day since the birthday before last
I have thought about my hair.

I began losing it soon after that birthday
and it has kept falling ever since.

They say it was a trauma that caused this—
probably one of the times I broke my face—

but I say it is something more mysterious
and insidious, like age.

Either way, it won't stop, this shedding,
this flowing-away,

this returning of my body
to the universe.

Oh—
but must every strand be taken?

Might I not be left a patch of wholeness,
a bit of unmarred beauty as a remembrance?

One by one, the leaves drop in their glory,
stealing the last of this October day.

Why this way?

Why must I witness each singular loss
as if my vigilance could stop the undertow?

Which part of me—watcher or watched—
will be last to go?

Now and Then I Give Myself
a Talking-To

Don't dwell on the fickleness of the past—
I say to myself in the mirror—

bring your thoughts
to the one certain thing.

Think of it when you start to feel sorry
for yourself, and think of it

when you are happy: its dark flavor
will intensify your joy. Yes—

remember it as much as you can,
let yourself be filled with it.

And when you overhear the mustard weed
whisper to the vetch,

*Yellow and purple, purple and yellow,
aren't we the beauties of the hill?*

think how the snow will cover their traces
and how dumb-lucky you are right now.

The Moth

Like bad neon, flickering
on the other side of the window,
a dozen moths are battering themselves
into the glass. They'll quit,
I suppose, when I put out the lights—
or when they're dead,
whichever comes first.

But one—a last-season holdover?—
has pinned himself to the pane,
and freezes, as I eye him,
into perfect camouflage:
The last yellowing leaves in the distance
are as small and delicate as mothwings,
almost as brittle.

Oh to age gracefully!
To press one's body
into the withering landscape
and fit in— I too
would try to hold my peace
if I didn't suspect that pose:
the only pose we hold unflinching,
our last.

Seven Infinities *of* Grief

Before and After

Clouds erupt in the enormous sky,
the kiawe fling their leaves into the wind—

Oh, how a thing is swept away
as one stands there, helpless,

watching the rain
through a calligraphy of trees

while a small, light-feathered bird
skims the surface of the rock—

a'a lava, sharp as steel, but brittle, bony—
then swoops up again and flies free.

Now another—white-winged and slender—
takes the same arc,

its topaz eye flashing a brilliant light
before it is gone.

Shivah: Grief's House

Door after door opens
and shuts.

One by one, the consolers enter,
and one by one, they leave.

The roses on the outer wall
release their dark music into the air,

which accepts each note completely
before letting it go,

while the bougainvillea splatters
its magenta on the pane,

breaking your heart because of all
you cannot help but remember.

Birds in a Dying Maple

But for their numbers,
you might not notice them:

sudden swoops of scarlet finches,
too many to be counted,

gathering on the limbs
of the naked tree.

Is it recompense
or merely consolation—

this burst of color, daring you
not to look back?

Enduring

Like awakening after a long illness
to find your health stole back in while you slept,

your sorrow, in its time,
will retreat,

and the knowledge you carried all along
will re-emerge, whole and cleansed.

One day you will not thrash in the too-bright light,
looking for a corner in which to close your eyes.

One morning the weight will not be there,
beneath your eyelids, the first thing you wake to;

it will not settle on your tongue
like a lump of salt.

And because you have stayed this long,
unrelenting, in the unrelenting world,

you know that time, though imperfect,
is diligent and wrestles down grief,

and that all things are born small
and grow large—

except grief, which is born large
and grows small.

Wind

It begins, you imagine,
as something captured—

a ball of azure atmosphere
or a pocket of light

pushing against its seams
until they split apart

and it rushes out in joy
to your window.

How the trees shake and sway,
letting loose their yellow, calling:

Let go the wreath of sadness
crowning your head.

You Do Not Belong to You

You belong to the universe
and you will be reclaimed

by its constant,
ever-changing heart—

your wise body
and your spacious mind,

when you are joyful
or not,

whether you are ready
or not,

even as you turn away
to be buffeted

and set aloft,
a twig in the wind.

Open Gate

The arc of evening
slowly rising,

the sun's blue shadows
washed away,

the gate still open
as three stars pierce the sky—

In the corridor, where night
bares its maze

you begin
to begin again.

With Gratitude

My thanks to the members of the Fort Bragg poetry group and to its organizer, Larry Felson, for helpful suggestions about earlier drafts of the poems. Thanks to Ken Fields and the members of his poetry workshop at Stanford, and to the members of the Berkeley Poets Co-op, from decades past. Thanks especially to Margaret Fountain Edwards and Erica Funkhouser, poet-friends from my Stanford days. Thanks to Anton Thuiliere for keeping everything organized.

My warmest thank you to Scarlet Tanager publisher Lucille Lang Day, fine poet and keen reader, with whom I've swapped poems for over five decades and who remains a dear friend today.

A big thank you to Bronwyn Becker, for her expert copyediting and wise counsel.

Very special thanks to my beloved friend Nancy Augustus, whose encouragement and support of every kind have kept me going.

To Steve Rood, my best reader and best friend, who has read every word in these pages countless times and made countless brilliant suggestions: Steve, it would take more pages than the book contains to thank you enough. I trust you know, more than my words can say.

Acknowledgments

My appreciation to the editors of the following magazines and anthologies, who have published my poems in earlier drafts:

American Poetry Review; *The Addison Street Anthology: Berkeley's Poetry Walk* (Heyday, eds. Robert Hass and Jessica Fisher); *Blue Arc West: An Anthology of California Poets* (Small Press Distribution, eds. Paul Suntup et al.); *Calyx: A Journal of Art and Literature by Women*; *Celebrating the Jewish Holidays: Poems, Stories, and Essays* (Brandeis University Press, ed. Steven J. Rubin); *Cloud View Poets, an Anthology: Master Classes with David St. John* (Arctos Press, eds. Morley Clark et al.); *Fire and Rain: Ecopoetry of California* (Scarlet Tanager Books, eds. Lucille Lang Day and Ruth Nolan); *Forward*; *Four Centuries of Jewish Women's Spirituality: A Sourcebook* (Beacon Press, eds. Ellen M. Umansky and Dianne Ashton); *Letters to the World: Poems from the Wom-Po Listserv* (Red Hen Press, eds. Moira Richards et al.); *Levure Littéraire*; *Lilith*; *Louisville Review*; *Nashim: A Journal of Jewish Women's Studies and Gender Issues*; *Poetry Flash*; *Prairie Schooner*; *Runes*; *September 11, 2001: American Writers Respond* (Etruscan Press, ed. William Heyen); *Shirim*; *Telling and Remembering: A Century of American Jewish Poetry* (Beacon Press, ed. Steven J. Rubin); *Women's Review of Books*; *Wrestling with Zion: Progressive Jewish-American Responses to the Israeli-Palestinian Conflict* (Grove Press, eds. Tony Kushner and Alisa Solomon); *Zyzzyva*.

About the Author

Marcia Falk is widely known in the progressive Jewish world for her poetic re-creations of Hebrew and English prayer. Her translation of the biblical Song of Songs is considered a modern classic. In addition to her books of poetry, she has published book-length translations of modern Hebrew and Yiddish women poets.

A lifelong artist, Marcia began art classes as a child at the Museum of Modern Art in New York and later studied painting at the Art Students League, where she is a Life Member. Her pastel drawing appears on the cover of this book. More of her art, as well as excerpts from her books, can be viewed at marciafalk.com.

Marcia grew up in metropolitan New York and now lives in northern California with her spouse, poet Steve Rood. Their son, Abraham Gilead Falk-Rood, teaches English and music to immigrant teenagers in a public high school.

Also from Scarlet Tanager Books

Bone Strings by Anne Coray
poetry, 80 pages

Fire and Rain: Ecopoetry of California
edited by Lucille Lang Day and Ruth Nolan
anthology, 462 pages

Poetry and Science: Writing Our Way to Discovery
edited by Lucille Lang Day
poetry and essays, 72 pages

The Rainbow Zoo by Lucille Lang Day
illustrated by Gina Aoay Orosco
children's book, 26 pages

Wild One by Lucille Lang Day
poetry, 100 pages

The "Fallen Western Star" Wars: A Debate About Literary California
edited by Jack Foley
essays, 88 pages

Catching the Bullet & Other Stories by Daniel Hawkes
fiction, 64 pages

Luck by Marc Elihu Hofstadter
poetry, 104 pages

Visions: Paintings Seen Through the Optic of Poetry
by Marc Elihu Hofstadter
poetry, 72 pages

Embrace by Risa Kaparo
poetry, 70 pages